SEEKING KINGDOM
ALPHABET BOOK

Shakeidra A. Reaux

Illustrated by - Katerina R. & Sheldon Moffett

All scriptures quotations, unless otherwise indicated,
are taken from BibleGateway- Amplified Bible (AMP)
© 2024 Shakeidra A. Reaux. All rights reserved.
Paperback/ 978-2-7015-2320-0
Hardcover/ 978-2-4598-8932-0
Ebook/ 978-2-7473-6935-0

SEEKING KINGDOM

ALPHABET BOOK

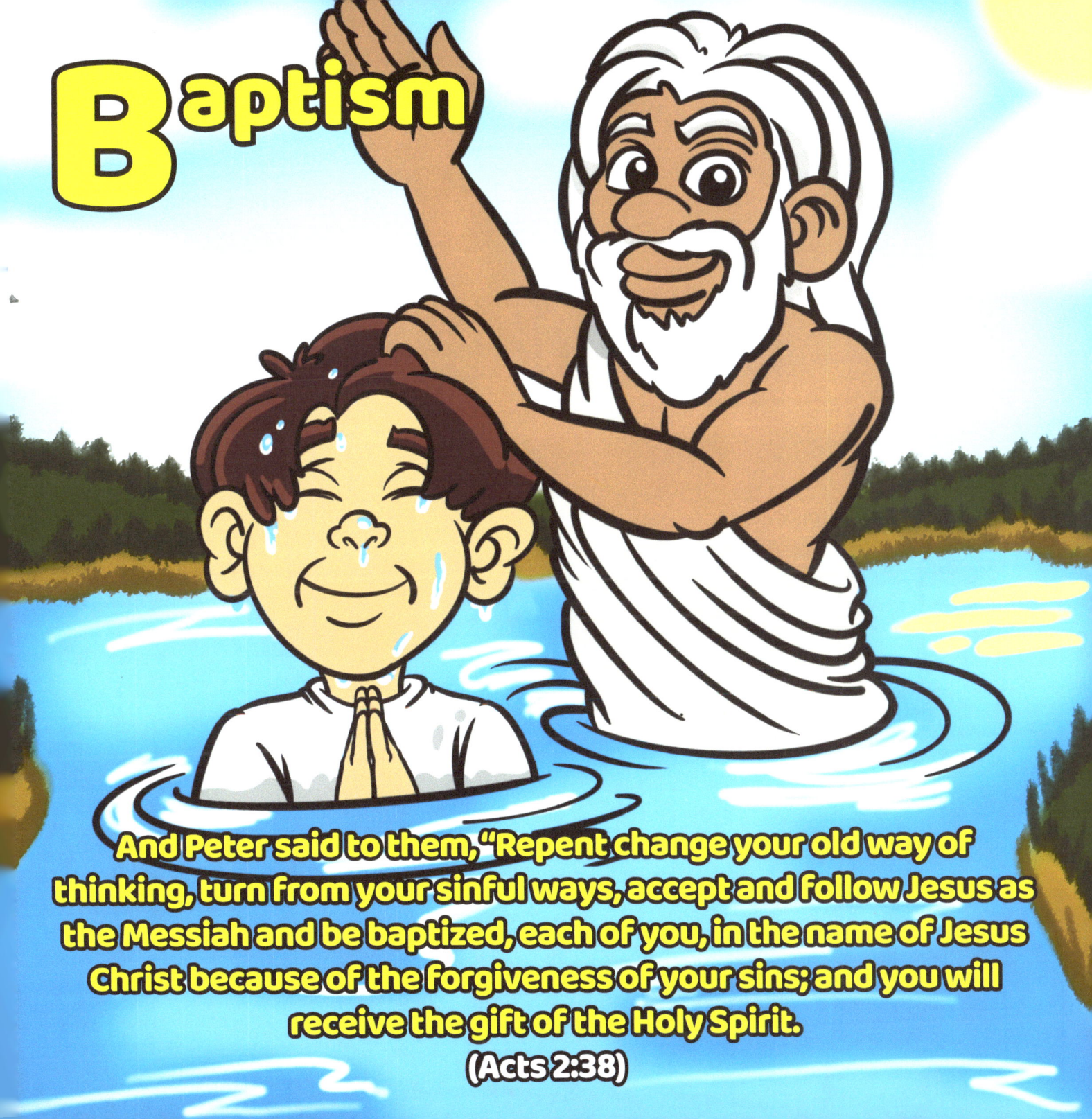

10 Commandments

If you really love Me, you will keep and obey My commandments. (John 4:15)

1. Put God first
2. Praise and worship him only
3. Keep God's name Holy
4. Keep the Lord's Day special
5. Obey your parents
6. Do not harm anyone
7. Love the one you Marry
8. Don't take anything that is not yours
9. Tell the Truth
10. Don't be jealous of what others have

Deliverance

When the righteous cry for help, the Lord hears and rescues them from all their distress and troubles. (Psalm 34:17)

Eternal

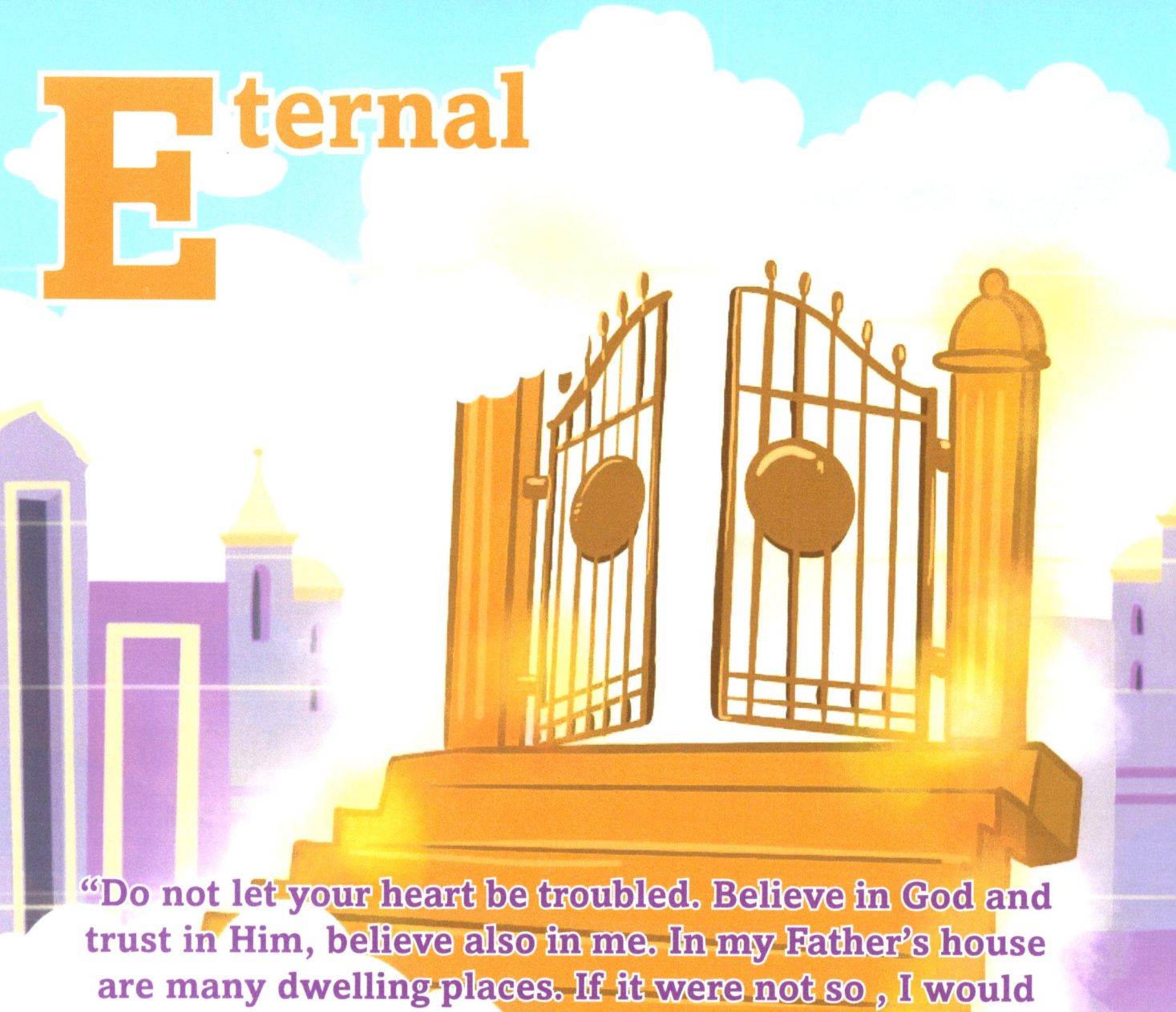

"Do not let your heart be troubled. Believe in God and trust in Him, believe also in me. In my Father's house are many dwelling places. If it were not so , I would have told you, because I am going there to prepare a place for you. And if I go and prepare a place for you, I will come back again and I will take you to myself, so that where I am you may be also. **(John 14:1-3)**

God

Do not fear anything, for I am with you; Do not be afraid, for I am your God. I will strengthen you, be assured I will help you; I will certainly take hold of you with My righteous right hand a hand of justice, of power, of victory, of salvation.
(Isaiah 41:10)

A woman in the crowd had suffered from a hemorrhage for twelve years, and had endured much suffering at the hands of many physicians. She had spent all that she had and was not helped at all, but instead had become worse. She had heard reports about Jesus, and she came up behind him in the crowd and touched his outer robe. For she thought, "if I just touch his clothing, I will get well." Immediately her flow of blood was dried up; and she felt in her body and knew without any doubt that she was healed of her suffering.
(Mark 5:25-29)

Trumpet

The first angel sounded his trumpet, and there was a storm of hail and fire, mixed with blood, and it was hurled to the earth, and a third of the earth was burned up, and a third of the trees were burned up, and all the green grass was burned up.
(Revelation 8:7)

1st

Trumpet

2nd

The second angel sounded his trumpet, and something like a great mountain blazing with fire was hurled into the sea; and a third of the sea was turned to blood; and a third of the living creatures that were in the sea died, and a third of the ships were destroyed.
(Revelation 8:8)

Trumpet

The third angel sounded his trumpet, and a great star fell from heaven, burning like a torch flashing across the sky, and it fell on a third of the rivers and on the springs of fresh waters. The name of the star is Wormwood; and a third of the waters became wormwood, and many people died from the waters, because they had become bitter.
(Revelation 8:10)

3rd

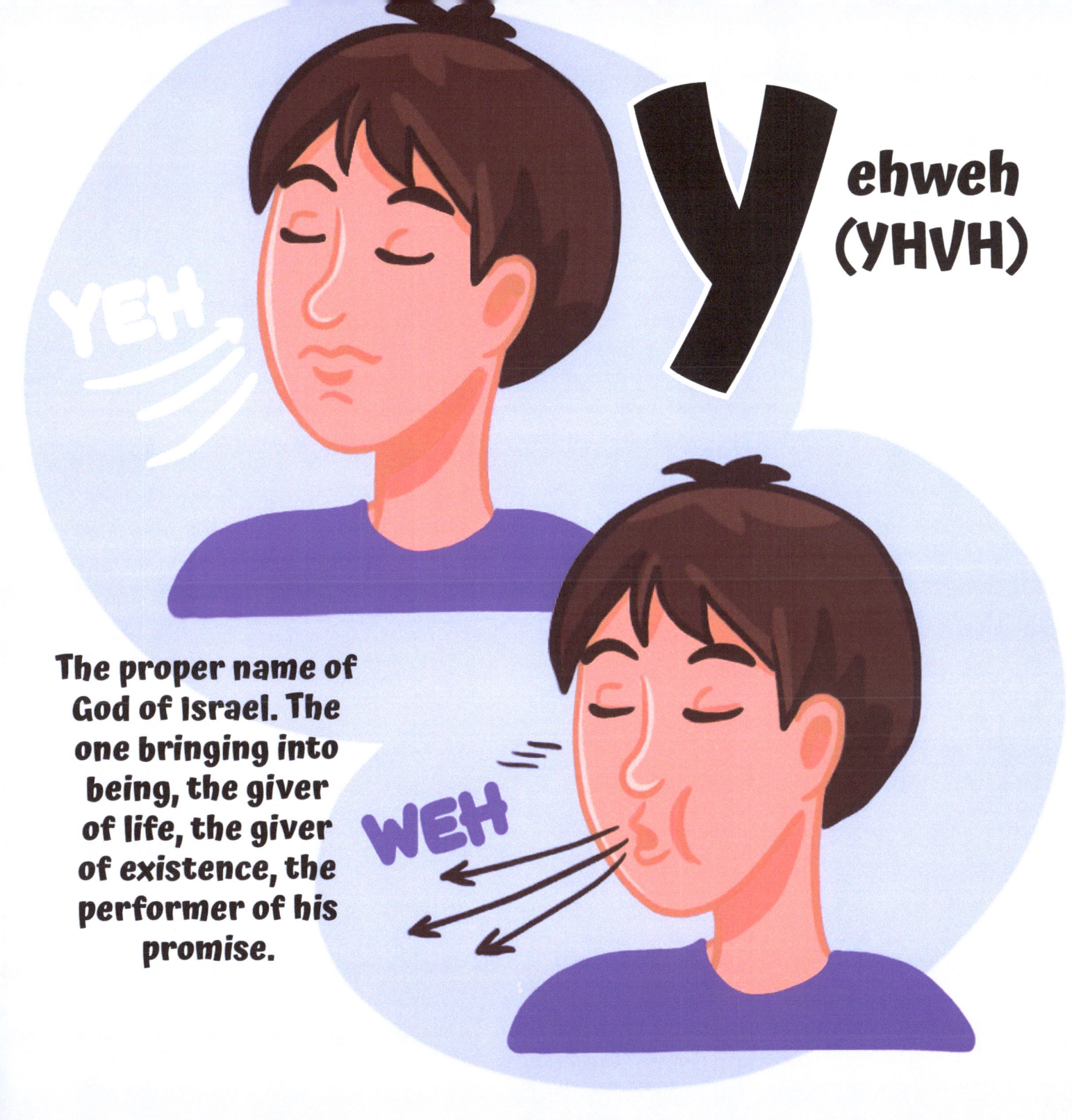

www.ingramcontent.com/pod-product-compliance
Lightning Source LLC
LaVergne TN
LVHW072251110526
838202LV00105B/2260